This book belongs to:
____

Tips for using this book:

1. Sit next to your grandchild as you do the pages together.
2. Identify & color the companion Chinese Zodiac animals.
3. Which animal stands for your birth years?
4. Which animal represents the current year?
5. Use crayons, markers, or colored pencils.
6. If pressing hard, place a sheet of paper behind the image.
7. Remove the pages, for ease of use, or if you're working with more than one grandchild.
8. Have fun as you color & do the fun activities!

Name each animal as you color. Where would you find each of these animals? Some live in the ocean, lake, river, forest, stream, jungle, woods, field, mountains, or lived in prehistoric times?

monkey
rooster
dog
pig
rat
bull
tiger
rabbit
dragon
snake
horse
sheep

Which animal stands for your birth years?

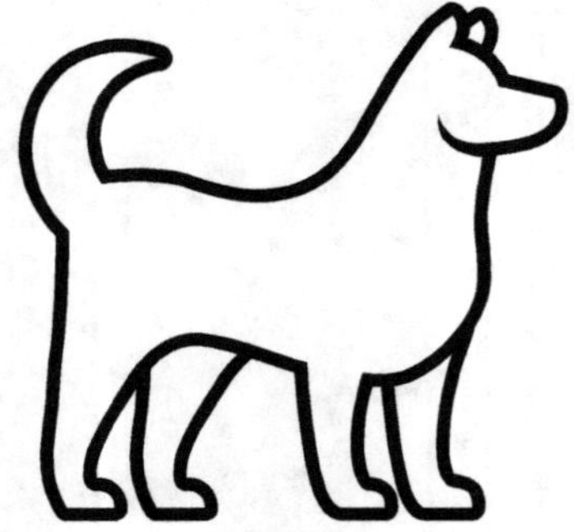

dog

horse

pig

snake

sheep

rat

monkey

tiger

rabbit

rooster

dragon

bull

Copy and color the picture

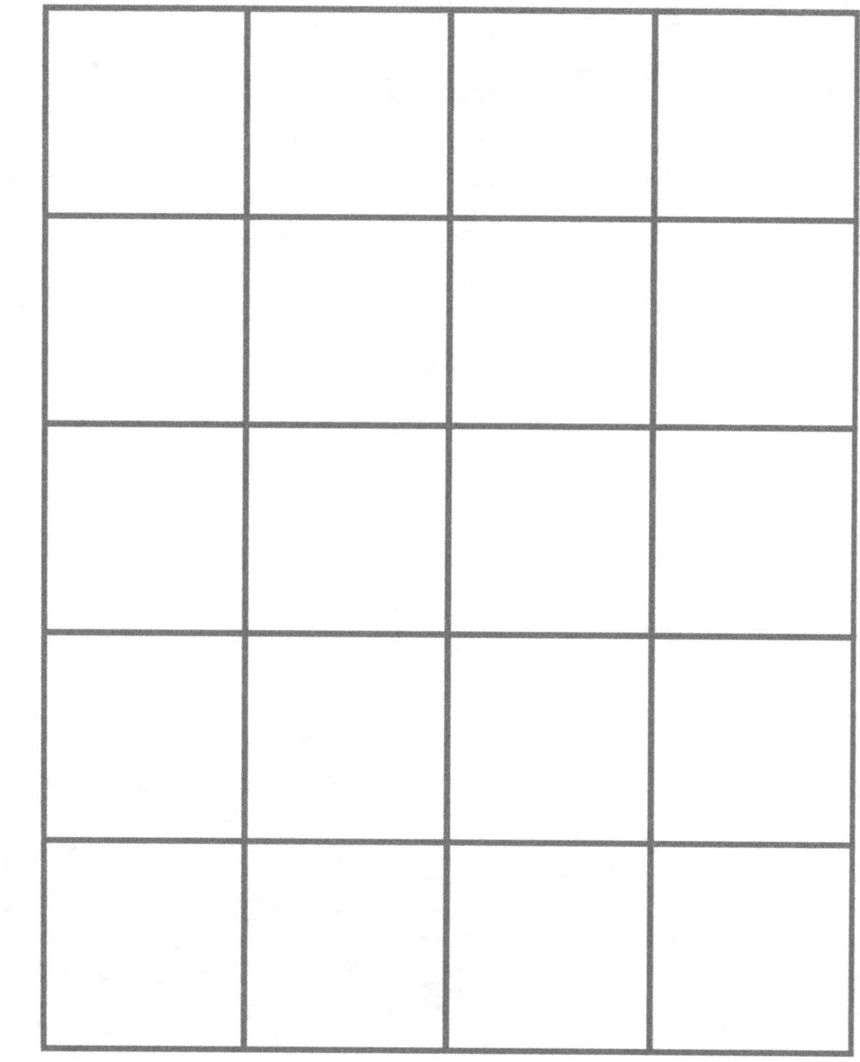

Copy and color the picture

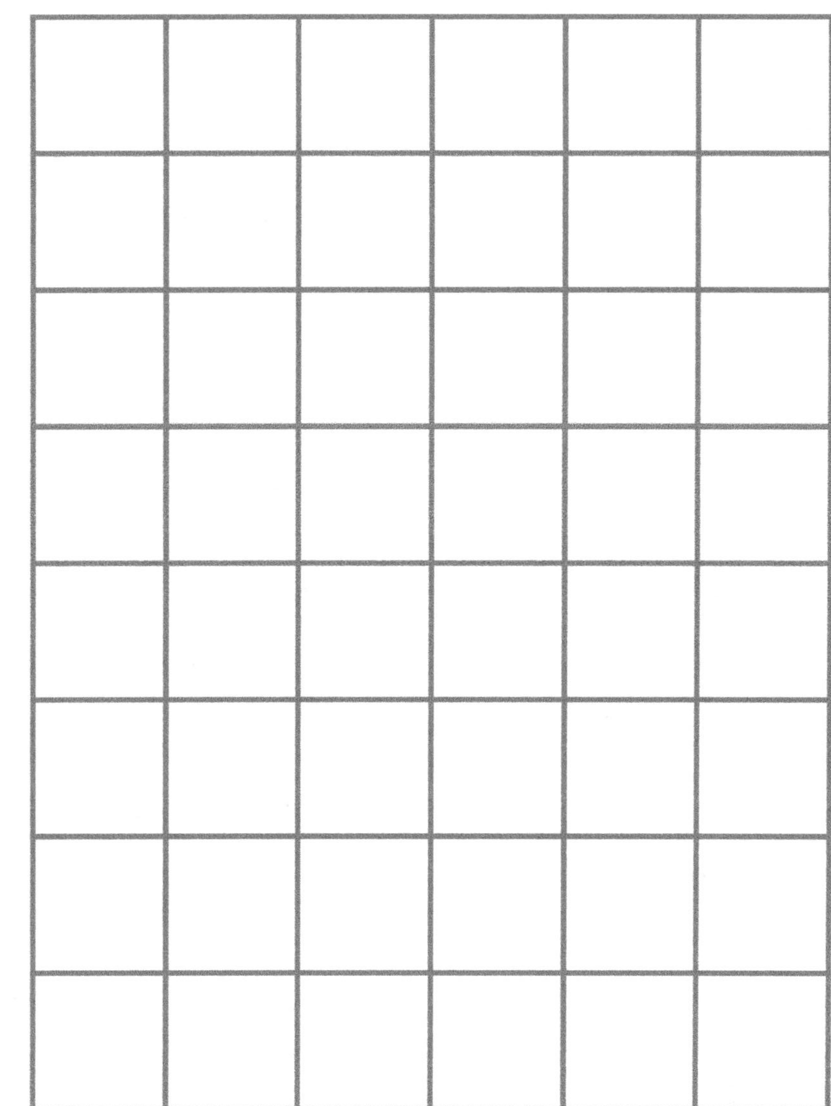

Copy and color the picture

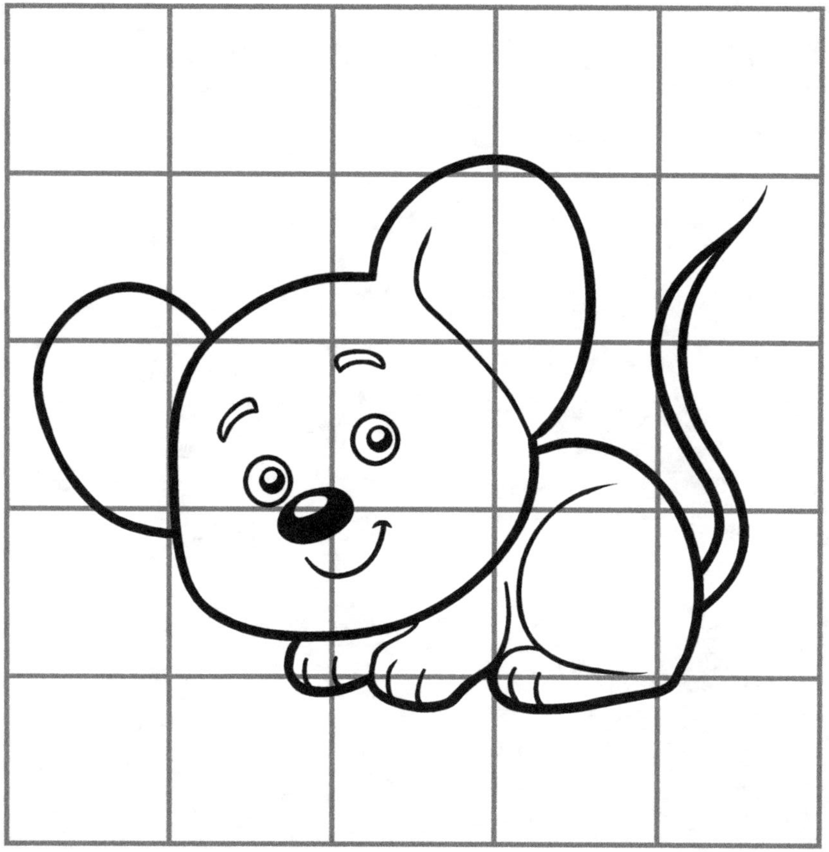

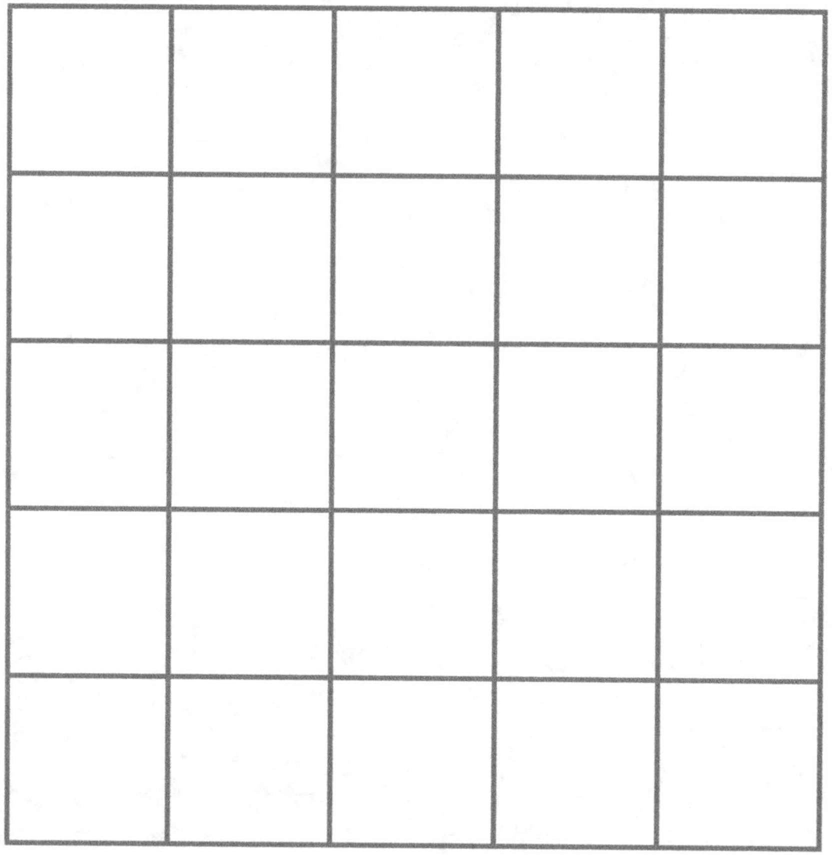

Copy and color the picture

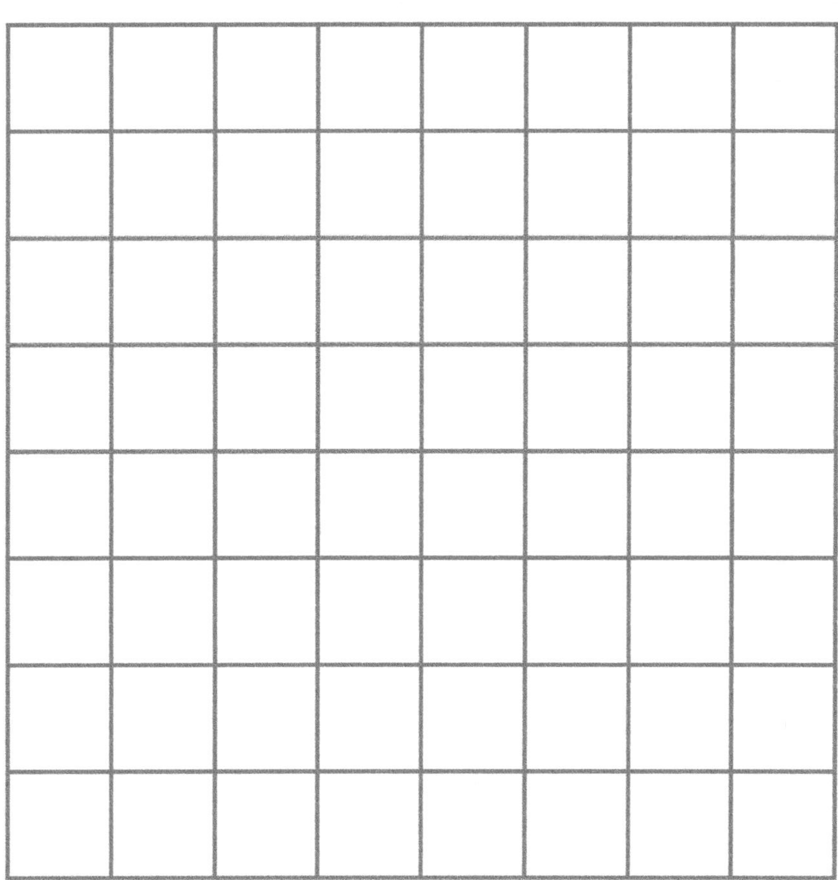

CUT & GLUE

COLOR — 1

CUT OUT — 2

GLUE — 3

USE EXAMPLE OR YOUR IMAGINATION

CUT & GLUE
COLOR
1
CUT OUT
2
GLUE
3
USE EXAMPLE OR YOUR IMAGINATION

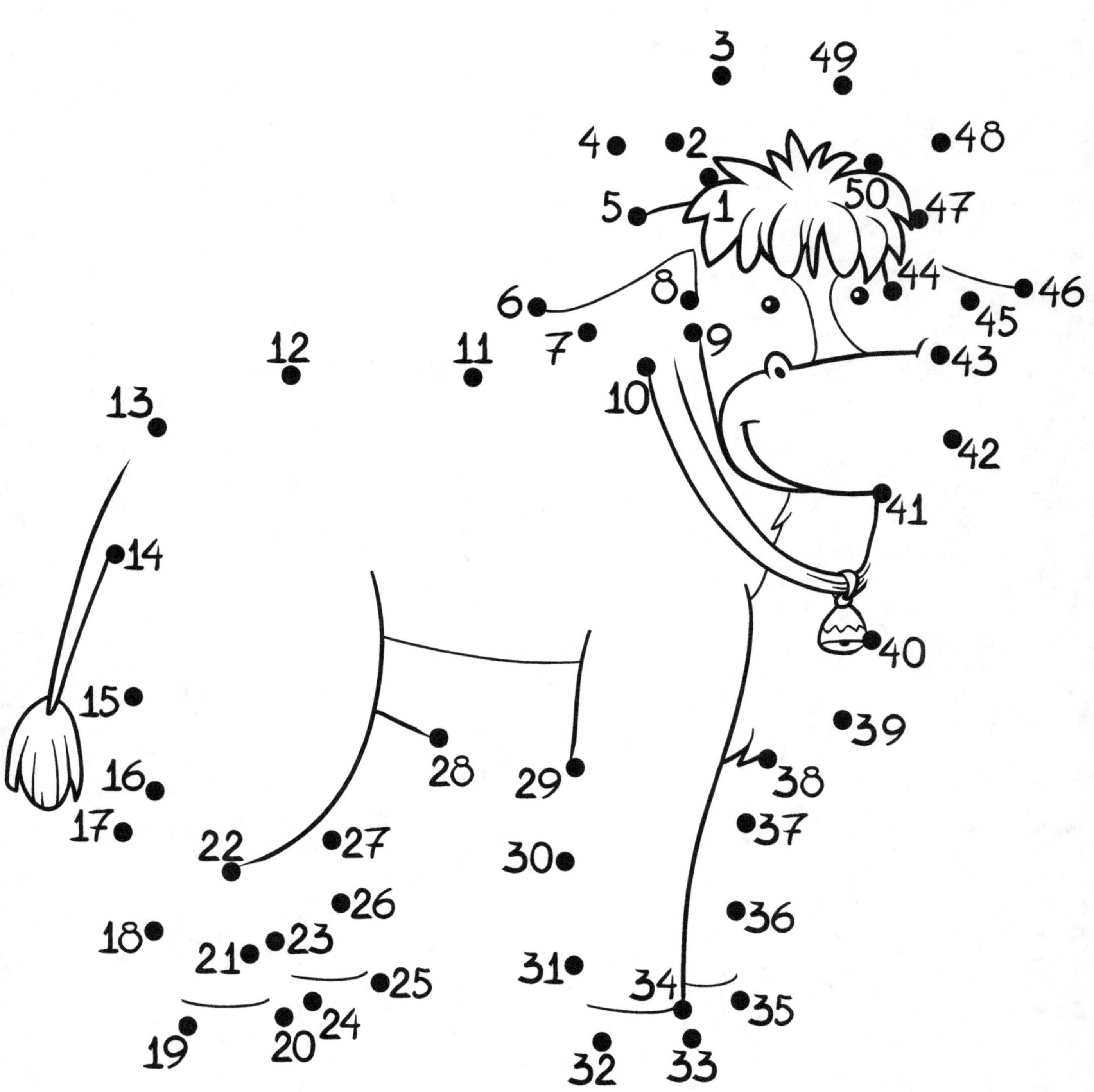

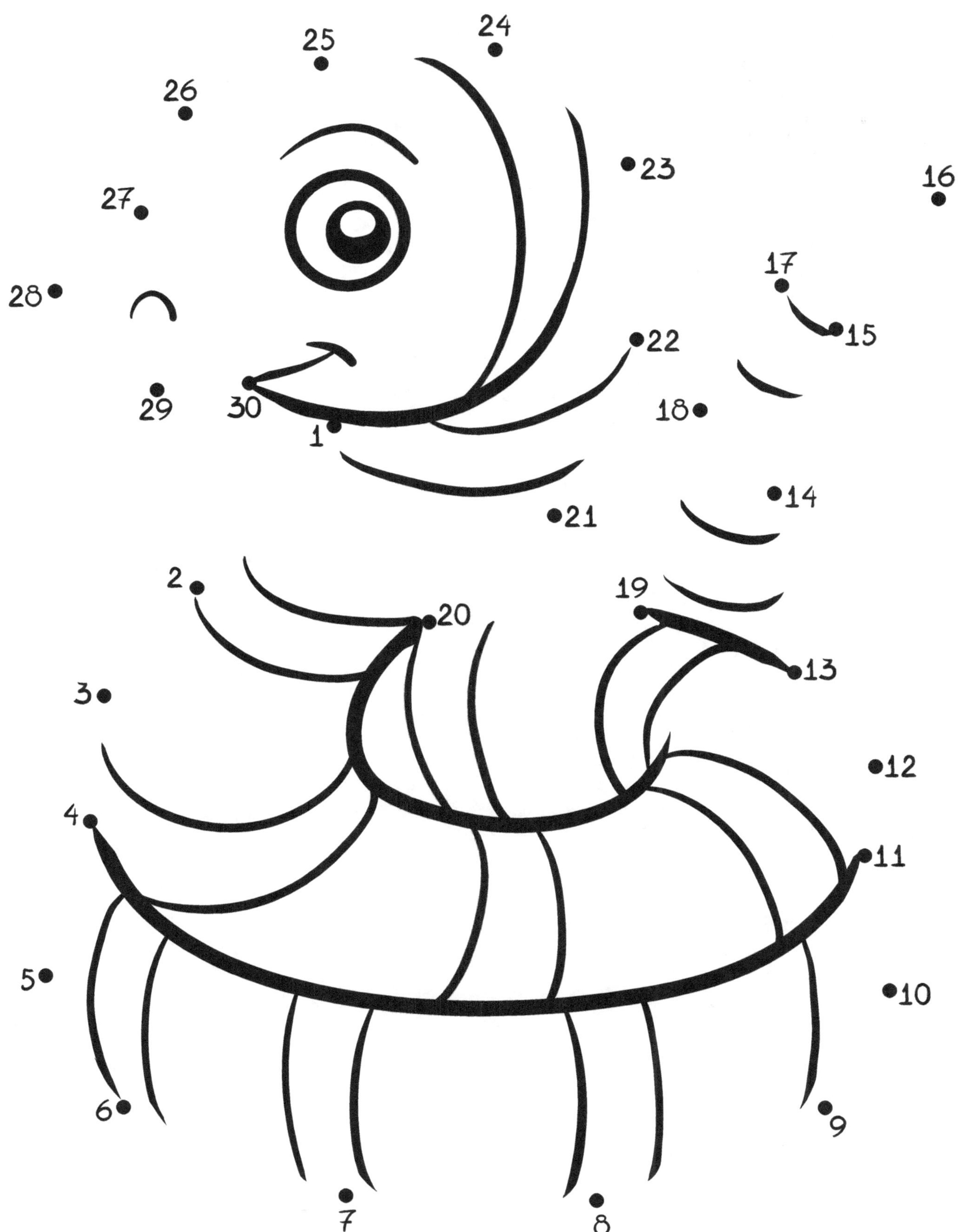

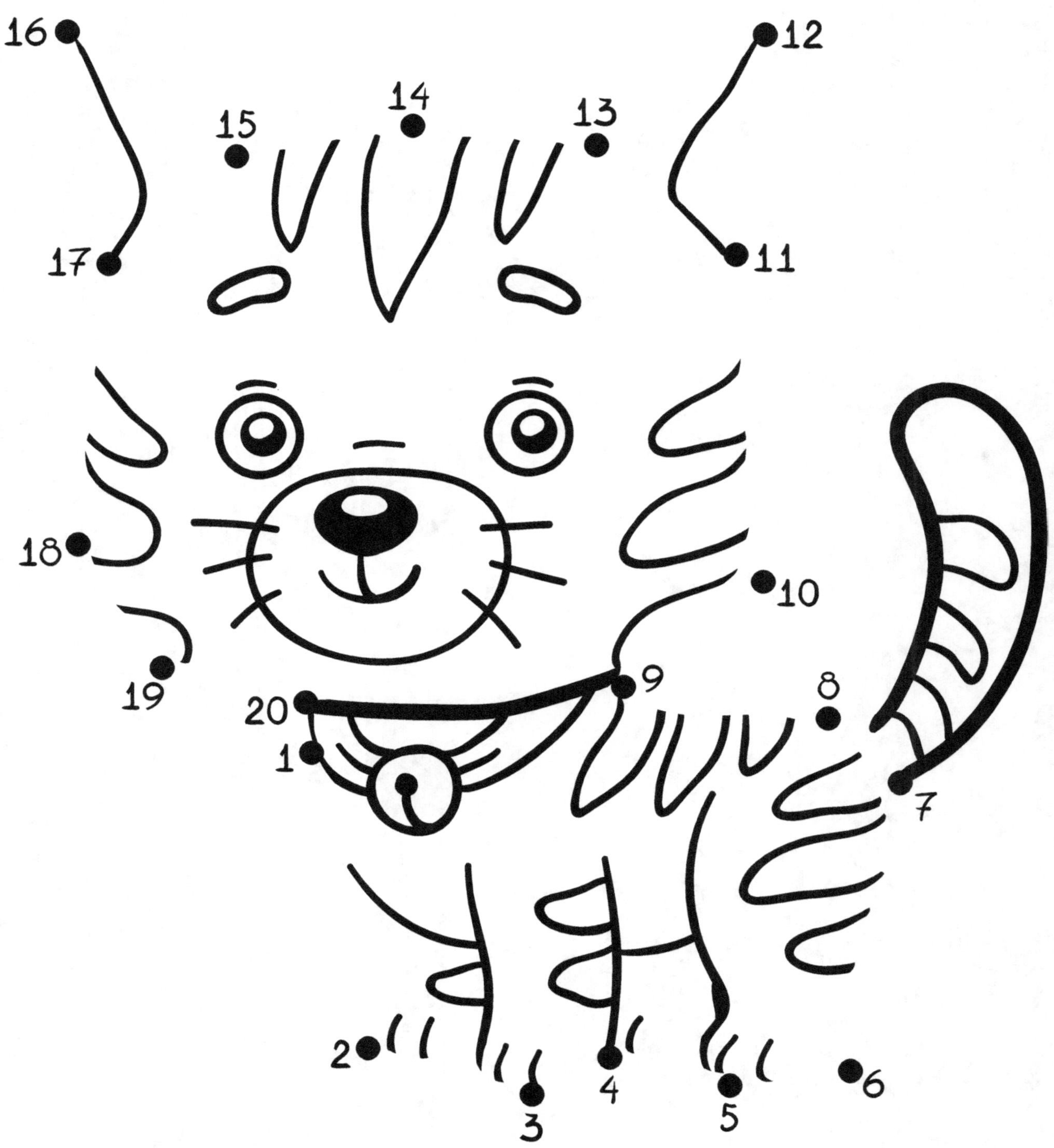

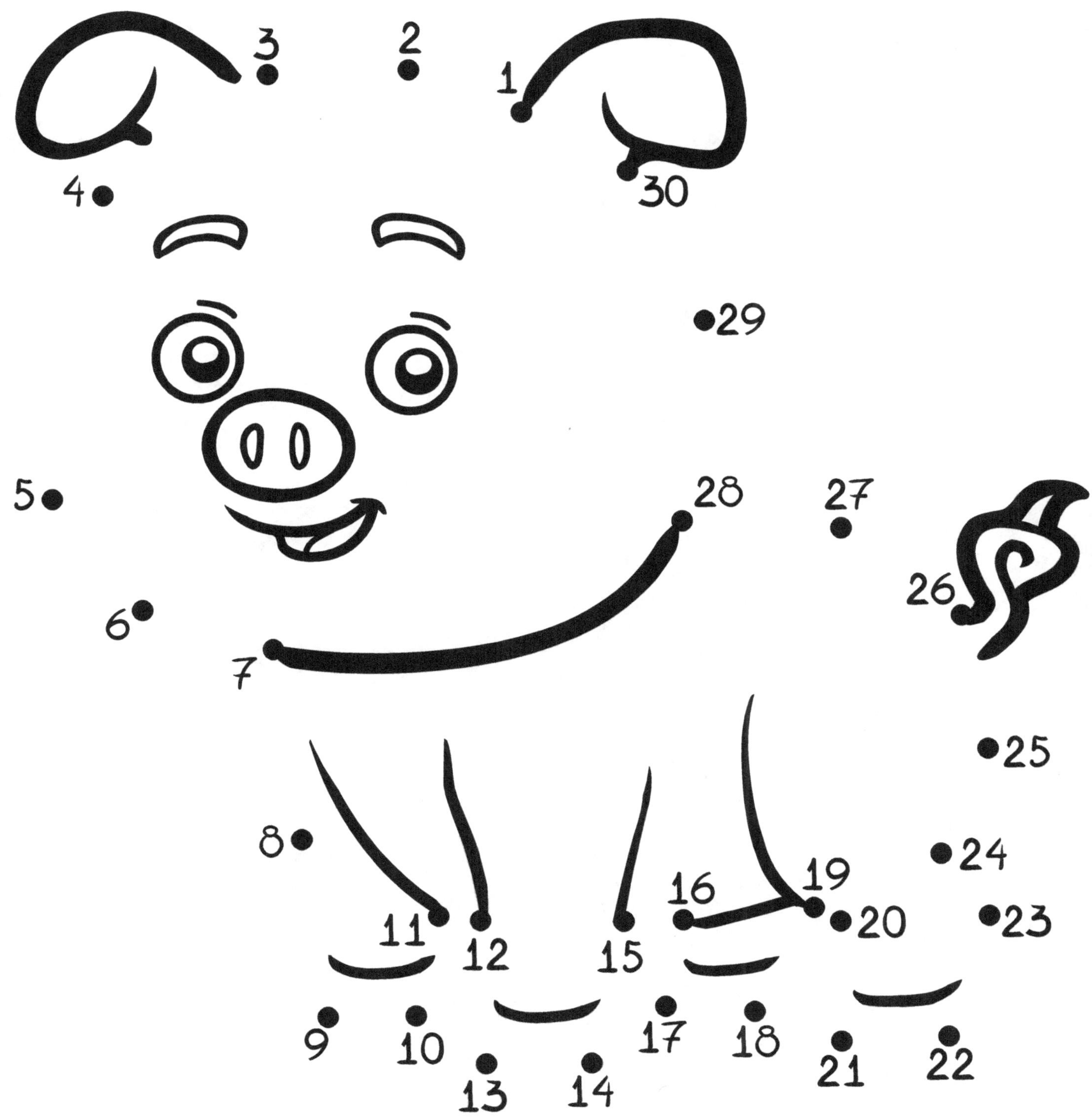

Color With Grandma! Chinese Zodiac Coloring & Activities for Children!
Copyright 2018 by Florabella Publishing, LLC

www.ingramcontent.com/pod-product-compliance
Lightning Source LLC
Chambersburg PA
CBHW081315250726
48662CB00008B/2584